Publishing eBooks Concept to Cash-Flow:

How to Publish your eBook on Amazon Kindle Step-by-Step from Start to Finish

by Christopher Kinkaid

 Solardyne.com

Published by Solardyne, LLC
Portland, Oregon

ISBN-13: 978-1500481810
ISBN-10: 1500481815

Table of Contents

Preface 3

About the Book 5

About the Author 8

Introduction 10

Chapter One: Content Publishing - the Big Picture 13

Chapter Two: Elements to Include 21

Chapter Three: Chapter Titles 29

Chapter Four: Formatting Text 35

Chapter Five: Formatting Images 43

Chapter Six: Creating your eBook Cover 47

Chapter Seven: The Importance of an Editor 51

Chapter Eight: Uploading your Document 53

Chapter Nine: Monetization 57

Chapter Ten: Building your Brand 61

Chapter Eleven: Publish Translations 65

Chapter Twelve: Overview Quick Guide to Steps 67

Preface

Learn how to format, and publish your eBook on Amazon Kindle in 19 Easy Steps, from Start to Finish. Digital publishing is a revolution - your Revolution.

Publishing eBooks is Easy, and Fast - if you know how. The most powerful communications tool on the internet, enables you to publish your eBooks, on the worldwide Amazon Kindle platform - and get paid. Reach marketplaces for your eBook around the world, all at once, using this Easy Step-by-Step guide.

Tap into the potential of reaching a worldwide audience for your eBook, to monetize your digital content, and generate monthly cash-flow. This eBook shows you how to format, and publish your eBook with the largest digital publishing platform on the planet. Bring your eBook from Concept to Cash-flow.

This Book goes Step-by-Step through the "Mechanics" of formatting, and publishing your eBook with a sequence of steps from Start to Finish.

Publishing an eBook is a complicated matter. There are proper conventions, formats, procedures, methods, and tools available, but how do you get through all the haze?

This Book is designed to bring you logically, and easily, step-by-step through the eBook publishing process, from Start to Finish in easy to follow steps. Reaching a worldwide audience is powerful tool for Authors, and Publishers. Learn how to Easily publish your eBook directly from your computer, to reach out and touch the world.

Publishing and distributing your eBook worldwide - is the greatest opportunity for Authors in the 21st century. This eBook is written to take you, and your eBook, from Concept to Cash-Flow, Step-by-Step, from Start to Finish.

About the Book

Use this Book to learn how to publish your eBook to Amazon in 19 Steps. This Book is written as a step-by-step procedure for formatting, and publishing your eBook to the worldwide Amazon Kindle marketplace, for worldwide distribution, and sale.

Publishing an eBook is complex in detail, but simple in format. Don't be intimidated, a mountain is climbed one step at a time. In eBook publishing, every issue has an answer. Every challenge, has a solution. Every eBook worth reading, should be written. Publishing your eBook to the world, with one click, gives you the power to reach a worldwide audience.

This Book is designed to take you from your eBook concept, through building a fully functioning dynamic eBook, and uploading your eBook to Amazon from Start to Finish. Take advantage of modern eBook features, and publish a useful, interesting, and pleasurable eBook experience for your readers.

Going from Concept to Cash-flow, these steps are the tools to access the greatest opportunity in modern communications: digital publishing from your Computer, directly to the worldwide Amazon network - in one click.

Use the **Quick Guide** with clickable links in Chapter Twelve which gives you a Step-by-Step check list for all of your elements, and formatting tasks.

Writing a successful eBook is more than just great writing. Publishing an eBook gives you the ability to reach global audiences, almost instantly, once you know how to do it. This Book covers the sequence steps, and technique for publishing your work from beginning to end.

Chapter 1 gives you the big picture, and reviews the design process for building your eBook

Chapter 2 outlines the Sections, or elements you should include in your eBook. The reader experience is the most important objective of digital publishing.

Chapter 3 discusses your eBook Title. The title defines your eBook not only for readers, but for the computer programs that rank your eBook.

Chapter 4 describes all of the formatting elements you need for modern eBook function.

Chapter 5 covers proper image formatting. Bring beauty and expression to your eBooks with Images, but insert, and save these images for true WISIWIG display in mobile devices.

Chapter 6 Production techniques for Creating your eBook Cover

Chapter 7 discusses the importance of having an editor. More eyes, means more insights on how your readers experience your eBook both emotionally, and intellectually.

Chapter 8 brings you to Uploading your files to Kindle publishing and going live on Amazon worldwide.

Chapter 9 covers monetization, setting pricing, getting paid, and generating monthly cash-flow.

Chapter 10 looks at building your brand. Now, that you're an Author, discover techniques to build your brand through increased web presence.

Chapter 11 discusses publishing books in different languages to increase the exposure, and number of eBooks you publish.

Chapter 12 is your Quick Guide, and Step-by-Step Final Check List

Use this Book to publish your eBook in easy to follow steps from eBook concept, through worldwide sales, and the production of monthly cash-flow.

About the Author

Christopher Kinkaid

Christopher (Toby) Kinkaid, originally from Portland, Oregon is the founder of **Solardyne.com**, **SolarQuote.com**, and **AlgaeToday.com**, and has worked in clean energy, and publishing technology for over three decades.

Kinkaid, is the inventor of the "Helyx" Vertical Axis Wind Generator, the "Mariposa" Non-imaging solar concentrator PV module (continuous operation at Sandia National Laboratory since 1994), the Solar Demultiplexer optical solar concentrating lens (Dr. James/Sandia National Laboratory 1991), and the inventor of the original "Solar Power Pack" (Mother Earth News, "Littlest Utility" June/July, 2001).

Kinkaid, has lectured on clean energy technology around the world including "APEC", Bangkok, Thailand, 2003, "Energy Solutions World", Tokyo, Japan, 2003, The International Biomass Conference

(IBC), 2010, Minneapolis, MN, and the Algal Biomass Organization (ABO) Conference, 2010, Phoenix, AZ.

Christopher (Toby) Kinkaid, has appeared in interviews on KOIN TV, KGW TV, and "Sustainable Today" produced in Oregon, and has served on the board of directors for the National Hydrogen Association, in Washington D.C., 1993, the Japan Satellite Communications Company (JCNET), Fukuoka, Japan, 1994-95, and Algaedyne Corporation, St. Paul, MN, 2010-2013.

Kinkaid, presently serves as CEO of Solardyne, LLC in Portland, Oregon, where he continues his work in Solar, Wind, and Biomass Technology applications, research, and development.

Introduction

Learn eBook publishing, directly from your computer, in 19 Steps.

Few revolutions present such opportunities for writers, and authors as digital publishing. Since the beginning of the digital age, from the world wide web, through Search, Social Media, to Apps, digital publishing has opened enormous markets for the consumption of information. An author's ability to be distributed on a global marketplace, and be paid directly with monthly royalties, is truly powerful.

Publish, Distribute, and Sell your eBook worldwide from Your Computer, with no cost.

Using the Amazon platform, useful information in every discipline, through eBooks, is only a search-and-click away from half the population on Earth. Amazon's enormous world wide marketplace, and the tools they provide for publishers, enabled the greatest revolution in communications since the Quill, - Digital Publishing at a Click.

Digital Publishing is a revolution with a difference, it's Your revolution.

The enormous genius of the Amazon platform is the ability for consumers to purchase, and download interesting information with one click. Once people are connected to the Amazon network, and have their account information already in place, purchasing information is quick, easy, and comprehensive.

This Book is written to share with you, the next author to Publish on Amazon Kindle, the "tools," and the "sequence" of applying those tools to produce the highest quality digital eBook possible.

In broad strokes, publishing your eBook on Amazon will follow Five Major Categories:

Content
Formatting
eBook Cover Image
Front Matter information
Uploading to Amazon

This Book breaks these Five Major Categories into 19 specific steps, so you can easily move your project from Concept to Cash-flow. Once you've written your eBook draft, and formatted your eBook step by step, you'll be ready to go live worldwide making your eBook available for purchase globally.

Monetize your eBooks with publishing royalties from the Amazon platform. Publishing on Kindle, you'll choose your royalty rates of 35% or 70% of the sales price, depending on the sales price you choose for your eBook. Have your royalties sent by check, or EFT with monthly payments, if you reach Amazon's monthly payment threshold (sales volume per month).

Digital publishing with Amazon is a brilliant business model, for the simple reason your costs are extremely low (free), and your reach is global with the Amazon platform earning royalties paid directly to you. It's a new world, and publishing eBooks, a great way to reach a worldwide audience, and earn great returns while you do it.

Chapter One - Content Publishing the Big Picture

Publishing your eBook successfully, begins with the quality of your eBook. After the quality of your content, the next two *most* important aspects of your eBook will be your Title, and your choice of eBook Cover.

Although the title of this Chapter is Content, the "Context" in which you frame your "Content" will determine its importance, and impact on the reader. Your Title and eBook Cover will be the most overwhelming factor in being well read, as Readers have an emotional response to eBooks. Amazon readers will be draw in, or pushed out, based on these "first" impressions.

Browsing eBook buyers decide to purchase eBooks based, overwhelmingly, on how the Title and eBook Cover pique their interest.

As you begin writing your eBook draft, start with your Title. You can always update, or change it later, before you go live, but it's the logical starting point. You can improve your Title's "placement," in Amazon searches with Keyword-rich Titles.

For Example, I published an eBook titled "Solar PV Water Pumping." When I started writing the eBook I wanted to call it "Pump your Water with the Sun." After some consideration, I realized even though I had "Pump" and "Water" in my title, from a computer search engine point-of-view, those were the only search-friendly keywords in my title.

I went with "Solar PV Water Pumping," in the end, because it described my book subject, and *each* word in my title was a Keyword. It was an organic word which someone might use who was actually searching Amazon for a Solar PV Water Pump. In choosing Keywords, you must enter the "mind" of your reader, and think as they would.

My new choice of Title greatly increased my "Keyword Density."

Note: (This is helpful for computers who direct "searches" to content). When a Kindle reader searches Amazon, with any term related to your Title, we want them to find you. You want your eBook to come up "high on the page" at, or near, the top in the Amazon search results. Choosing your Title carefully is vital.

Titles, (and Sub-Titles) are so important **Chapter Three** is dedicated to the subject.

Once you have some titles sketched out, then put together an eBook Cover concept. You may ask, "why are we starting with the eBook Cover? Isn't that the cart before the horse?" The reason to start with your Title and eBook Cover is inspiration.

Note: **Chapter Six** covers eBook covers, but they're so important, thinking of them early is insightful, and fun. When I write an eBook I put a copy of my Cover on my desk while I'm writing. I find it inspiring through the writing process. It's exciting, and gives me my goal in the process. And, as I write, I continue to "evolve" on the Cover graphics. As my eBook grows, so do the graphics. Writing is organic, you'll end up, often, far away from where you started, but isn't that what a great journey is all about?

Research the Amazon Market for Keywords, and eBook Covers

Search Amazon for eBooks in, or near, your subject matter. Look at the eBook covers which come up in your search.

Which search terms brought up the most "accurate" eBooks? What draws your eye? What pulls you in? What makes you think "I want more?"

Writing an eBook is hard work, and requires the best of your abilities. Writing is best when you "surf" the waves of your passion. Passion involves high energy, and your subject-content is the heart of your power in publishing - draw on your passion.

Creating your eBook cover is really exciting to look at, and always gives me an emotional boost. Writing, Buying, and Reading eBooks is an emotional experience. Tap into this excitement, and you'll enjoy your writing as you follow these steps from start to finish.

Consider your Audience, and their Screens

Writers must make content interesting, and in a style which is easy to read on mobile devices. Writing eBooks, displayed on Mobile devices will have differences with traditional print book phrasing. Shorter phrases work best on small screens. Mobile screens are about 1/3 the size of desktop computer screens.

Writing "content" for eBooks is different than writing for traditional print books. Mobile devices, Smart Phones, Tablets, and other platform smaller screens change the reading experience.

Long paragraphs don't read as well on small screens. Writing in shorter paragraphs is not suggested to truncate your content, or poetic license, but rather to consider your platform, and maximize the Reader Experience.

The specific steps in Kindle eBook Digital Publishing listed in the last Chapter are written to give you a specific roadmap from start to finish. Use these steps when you begin your writing process, and you'll go from concept to cash-flow. When you're ready to launch your eBook on the worldwide Amazon platform please refer to **Chapter Eight** and upload your book files.

Writing your eBook - the Big Picture

Your eBook will begin as a simple WORD document. Use a plain font, and 12 pt. text. Kindle readers can chose their own font and font size when they read your eBook, so page numbers are non-existent, and obsolete to the mobile device reader. Don't worry about formatting in the beginning. You'll format your document near the end of the writing process (this will save you a lot of time in the end).

When you begin writing just start with a plain Word document using plain text font and size. Kindle is designed to receive "simple" Word documents which they convert into **.mobi** formats when they publish your eBook on their platforms. There is formatting you must do, in fact, very specific formatting, but doing this last will save you a lot of effort in re-editing.

The working draft of your eBook will be a WORD document with .doc extension. Write your eBook Without any formatting other than Hard Paragraph Returns separating the paragraphs within a single Chapter.

This "plain Jane" approach will save you time as you reach the end of the document.

Elements to include in your eBook:

In **Chapter Two**, below, all of the sections, or elements you should include. The elements are outlined and described. To generated a rough draft of your eBook, follow these easy steps.

The steps are designed in a sequence which makes "building" your eBook easier, and follows a logical flow. After you've written your eBook, you'll "build" the eBook stitching together your elements with hyperlinks. More on that later in Chapter Four: Formatting.

Digital Publishing Overview:

The large "Brush-Strokes" in digital publishing are to write Content, Format your Content, write your "Front Matter," produce your eBook Cover image, and register with Amazon publishing. Once you're registered, you'll log onto your "Bookshelf" page.

Your "Bookshelf" page is the launching platform from which you enter your eBook "Front Matter" information, and begin building your eBook.

To begin the eBook publishing process, select NEW TITLE, on your Amazon Bookshelf page.

Front Matter refers to all of the "supporting" information around your eBook. Title, Sub-title, Author, or other contributors are listed, declaration of your copyright to your material, descriptions, keywords, categories which most closely match your subject, are all included in "Front Matter" information.

You'll need to prepare three basic parts of your eBook. The "Front Matter" information, described above. The eBook itself, formatted properly, and your eBook Cover Image file.

Upload your Content (.doc) files, and eBook Cover image (.JPEG) file under your New Title. Once Uploaded onto the Amazon Kindle platform, you'll select the dollar (or other currency) amounts you wish to charge for each copy, for each territory, or worldwide, and click SAVE and SUBMIT.

Once you Submit your files, you go live - worldwide - in 12 to 48 hours.

From your computer, you have the ability to publish worldwide with Amazon publishing. There is no charge from Amazon to sell eBooks on their network. For authors, and publishers, the Amazon publishing platform is a revolution in empowerment. Anyone, anywhere can reach out and touch the world.

In the following chapter, we'll go Step-by-Step through the separate "Elements," you'll use in "building" your eBook on Kindle.

Chapter Two - Elements to Include in your eBook

When you're finished writing the final draft of your eBook, the "content" of your eBook will be formatted for digital download.

As such, your best approach is to have a rich Selection of Elements included in your eBook format, and take advantage of the special features of eBooks. Different sections, or elements, give your reader several ways to look at your eBook, Navigate your ebook, find information about the eBook, and provides a rich environment for enjoying your eBook.

Readers who buy eBooks are looking for ease of use, depth of content, and enjoyment in the eBook experience. Navigating eBooks is a big feature for readers. Each of your sections will be directly available to your readers by simply "clicking" on hyperlinks you'll put in your Table of Contents, and special places in your text.

Properly formatted eBook functions are vital for a successful eBook. Chapter 4 (Formatting) will cover the essential formatting features expected in modern eBooks.

In an eBook, the "Table of Contents" is dynamic. Chapter Titles, are clickable taking you directly to the start of the Chapter in the body text, or other Section, as the reader chooses.

Elements to include in your eBook, in this case, refer to "packages" of specific information which help the reader navigate your eBook. Different sections, listed below, are designed to "group" information about your eBook giving your reader many options.

Each major element will have it's own dedicated page, or pages, and place in your Table of Contents.

In the formatting section, Chapter 4, we'll go through the hyperlinks, bookmarks, and other formatting requirements. Hyperlinks give your reader instant links to other relevant parts of your book, or directly to websites. Sections in your eBook, give your reader "larger brush strokes" on how information in your content is organized.

Writing your eBook with these elements give your readers a more complete view of the Author, Book Content, and serves to improve the reader experience.

Step 1: Writing your "Table of Contents"

Writing, or Reading, an eBook all starts with the Table of Contents. If you're just starting to write your eBook, start with the Table of Contents. Writing the "Table of Contents" first, gives you a writer's "roadmap" to your own eBook, and helps organize your Chapters.

As you begin writing your Table of Contents, it forces you to think of your eBook in broad strokes, and as a process. Listing Chapter Titles, or proposed titles, give you a basic structure to the progression of your eBook. As you begin writing your eBook you can follow your Table of Contents and work on one Section, or Chapter at a time.

How do you eat an Elephant? One little bite at a time. The same is true with writing eBooks. It's easy to feel overwhelmed when facing the "mountain to climb" of writing an eBook. However, if you write your Table of Contents first, you can focus on one little "bite" easing the burden of the whole project.

The Table of Contents is the "Grand Central Station" of your eBook. The Table of Contents gives your readers access to any part of your eBook by clicking your hyperlinks.

Step 2: Writing your "Preface"

The "preface" gives your eBook reader an overview of your eBook topic, and what they can expect in purchasing your book. Write your preface in a style of positive, and informative script, with the intension of some seduction.

The "preface" you write should offer some excitement and enticement to the reader. Describe what the reader will discover, and gain in reading your eBook. The "preface" can also work as an introduction to the introduction (another section). In the "preface" give the largest "context," or "perspective" to your book. The "preface" should be the "hook" which leaves your reader wanting more. Write your "preface" as if you are the reader, and you want to be romanced.

Step 3: Writing your "About the Book"

The "About the Book" section is important, and written to give a "mechanical" overview of the eBook. Include chapter descriptions, and insights to be gained by the reader in each chapter. The "About the Book" section is a "user manual" for navigating your eBook, and giving the reader a "short-hand" view of your eBook.

Step 4: Writing your "About the Author"

This section "About the Author" is vital to building your brand. Readers want to know *who* is writing this eBook, and, probably third most important in their buying decision, after Title, and eBook cover. You're writing an eBook because you have something to say. You have something to add to the literature, and therefore, you must publish. The "About the Author" section should include highlights of your career, or background, which qualify you as the writer.

Credibility comes from your experience. Your section "About the Author" can include your photo, (make sure your image is just of you, head-shot, and professional quality). Include any website URLs you may have related to your eBook subject. If you've published other websites include those as part of your experience.

Step 5: Writing your "Introduction"

The "introduction" of your eBook is important in setting the tone, and scope for the reader. Non-fiction, or fiction, in all cases the introduction sets the stage, for your "digital production" and sets the "context" to give perspective to your "content."

Your "introduction" section should build on your "preface" and explore the large issues bringing the focus into, or "down," from your subject to your topic. Include the largest "context" of your topic, and bring the reader into the specifics. If you're writing a Fiction, then your introduction sets the scene, and brings the reader into your story from the outside. If you're writing a Non-fiction, the introduction frames your eBook topic, and mentions exciting, or titillating aspects to a normally potentially dull subject.

Step 6: Writing your "Chapters"

Organize your eBook in separate Chapters for the body of your text, and images if you include them, taking your readers on a journey. The number of Chapters is variable, and depends on your eBook content. Chapters are instantly accessed by the reader from the "Table of Contents" in eBooks with hyperlinks. Naming your Chapters is important keeping in mind the smaller screen formats of portable devices. Although Kindle users can adjust the Size of the text being displayed in the Kindle readers, Chapter Titles in your Table of Contents are generally best kept short, and to the point.

Keeping your Chapter Titles shorter in your "Table of Contents," but longer in the Chapter Titles as displayed in the "body" of your text gives your eBook a clean look. This keeps your "Table of Contents" uncluttered, yet keeps your actual Titles in the "body" of your eBook more explanatory and true to your original intent. When you get to the Formatting steps, format your Chapter Titles and Sub-Titles as Heading 1 in your WORD styles drawer.

Chapters should separated by Page Breaks, inserted in your WORD.doc document. This will be covered in Chapter Four - Formatting.

Step 7: Writing your "Epilogue"

Readers always have an emotional, and intellectual experience with an eBook. Excitement, frustration, it can run the gambit through the reading experience. An "epilogue" is a nice technique to "bring your reader" down, and paint in broad strokes. The "epilogue" puts a period at the end of the sentence, so to speak, and wraps up the meaning of your conclusion, and revisits what the reader has just experience. Sum up the experience in your Epilogue.

Chapter Three: Writing your eBook Title

The two most important aspects of your eBook, after the Quality of your Content, is your Title, and eBook Cover.

Drafting your title will go through several stages. Begin with the Title in your heart, the short phase, or name, which goes to the meaning, and essence of your eBook. This is your "romantic" version of the Title.

In digital publishing, Titles for eBooks, have two parts: the Title, and Sub-title.

Digital publishing is different from print publishing. Think of your eBook in two ways: from a "human", as well as, "computer" perspective. The first way to think about your eBook is from the human point-of-view.

The "human" way to think of your eBook is through the emotional, and intellectual, experience of your reader. The reader experience, includes how your title and cover inspire a buy decision as readers search for interesting eBook topics, and their excitement in wanting to read your eBook.

The second way you must think of your eBook, is in terms of how computers "think."

Digital publishing is on a digital platform. As such, computers are integral to how digital publishing operates.

From a computer's perspective the world is not seen in grey shades, it's only black and white. Most computer programs define the questions, and answers, a computer "considers" in any action. From the "perspective" of a computer program, how does your title look?

Are there any words in your title which allow a "search" to find your eBook? Are there any words in your title which a "human" may use in searching your topic? Computer search engines, including Amazon, can only direct people to content which "registers" in the computer programs.

Digital eBooks will be listed on "computer" based platforms. How your reader finds you depends, specifically, on how you describe your eBooks content in the Title, and Sub-title.

Do not use marketing ploys in your titles. As a rule, don't "pitch" your book in its title, such as "Best Seller," or "Number 1." Let accolades come, but titles are no place for marketing, it's the place for Description. Note: Sub-Titles, however, is the place for marketing.

In our two ways of thinking, the "human" title should be emotionally, and intellectually "descriptive" of your content. Let the meat of your eBook be the focus of the title.

From the "computer" perspective, you want your title to be composed of "search" words.

Avoid un-necessary words, or words which don't maximize your Readers' Understanding, and the computers ability to "recognize" your content. In the spirit of eBook writing, keep your titles Potent, and Rich in descriptive words. You want words that bridge the "human" and "computer" experience and provide useful effects in both worlds.

Step 8: Writing your Title, and Sub-Title

Writing successful, and effective Titles and Sub-titles, work best with some Research.

Pretend you're a reader, and log onto Amazon to browse the available Kindle eBooks. Get a feel for the content available, and pricing, not to emulate what you see, but to determine your own identity when you go live. Check out the "landscape" of related eBooks. Look at the Titles, Cover graphics, and Book Descriptions.

As you "search" for eBooks on Amazon, make note of what titles reach highest on the list. Did your "search" word appear in the title of the eBooks which comes up?

Titles are generally brief. However, write your Sub-title rich with "Keywords" which are searchable. In General your Title is Short, and your Sub-Title is longer, rich in Keywords. Researching "keywords" which people use for your topic is good to know. You can "test" your Keywords in a variety of ways, but the best way is "organic" research.

Organic research is when you make a list of "keywords," and search those words on the Amazon Kindle eBook platform. Do your "keywords" give you good results? As the author of your eBook, become familiar with the "landscape" of available literature. Searching Amazon as a Kindle Reader will greatly sharpen your market awareness, as well as help you in setting on your sale price.

In the example above I mentioned one of my eBooks "Solar PV Water Pumping." How I decided on high "keyword density" with this title choice.

My Sub-Title for "Solar PV Water Pumping" is "How to Solar Power Water Pumping Systems for Wells, Creeks, Ponds, Lakes, and Streams."

My Sub-Title is rich in additional, and different, Keywords giving the "computer" search engines something to grab. I have "How to" as a popular search element. In addition to my Title Keywords, I have Power, System, Wells, Creeks, Ponds, Lakes, and Streams. All of these words are "possible, and likely" search terms a potential Reader may use to find an eBook on my subject.

Choose your Title, and Sub-Title with great care, research, and consideration for successful response in both the "human" perception, and "computer" classification of your eBook.

Chapter Four - Formatting your eBook Text for Kindle Publishing

Formatting your eBook is important work. Perhaps the most fun aspect of writing an eBook, is the formatting step. Now, you've written your Final Draft, it becomes time to format your eBook for the worldwide market. Proper formatting is vital for a successful digital publishing experience.

The "fun," in formatting your eBook is seeing your eBook come into functioning form - it comes alive. Writing the first draft "body" of your eBook is done in plain text. In the formatting steps to follow, you'll bring your "vanilla" plain text draft document into the living world, with hyperlinks, and a fully functioning Table of Contents.

Hyperlinks will allow your eBook reader to jump around your eBook as you "link" different parts of your eBook. "Destinations" of your hyperlinks, are called Bookmarks.

It's best to do your formatting after you've written the body of your text. Write your book first, and save the formatting steps for last. The reason formatting your eBook near the end is logistics.

Writing is an organic process, and you will re-edit your text. If you set up your formatting too early, dollars to donuts, by the time you reach the end of your Draft, you'll be pulling your hair out trying to "clean" out all of your previous formatting. Trust me, save it for last.

Document files (your eBook draft) are "uploaded" to the Kindle Digital Publishing network in several preferred formats. These preferred formats include PDF, HTML, HML and WORD document files. The preferred format to use are WORD document files.

For a smooth Uploading experience write your eBook using MS WORD either with .doc, or, .Xdoc file extensions (when you save the document). If you're using a Mac, then save your documents under SAVE AS, Name, and select WORD.doc file format.

Step 9: WORD documents

Kindle is designed to make publishing as easy as possible. Writing your eBook begins with your WORD.doc file.

To begin writing your eBook, start with a plain WORD.doc in your MS WORD processor, and Name your file. The formatting required by Kindle is relatively simple, but must be precise.

Note: Don't use your Headers, and Footers function. Leave these blank, and be sure they are in the same font as the body of your text. To check, just click on the header, or footer in your document, and the font will be displayed. You want your entire WORD.doc document to be in one font. My personal preference for font is Myriad Pro @12 point.

Kindle supports Tables, in your Word document. If you wish to use "Tables," then "Insert" your tables with the Insert pull down menu on your Function bar. You can use character formatting, such as Bold, Italic, and indents. Note: I recommend you DO NOT use Bold, Italic, or Indents. In formatting conversion, this is where formatting errors can be introduced, so avoid these character formats. Just use plain text.

Note: Don't adjust character "sizes" in your word document using the Sizing function. Use the Headers 1, and Headers 2, covered below, if you want to make Titles, and Sub-Titles in your text pronounced.

Step 10: Inserting Page Breaks

The Kindle format is very specific for Page Breaks. Page Breaks dictate how Chapters are separated in your document.

Using your "Insert - Page Break" function key, insert a Page Break at the end of each Chapter. This insures there are no extra spaces, or extraneous Hard Returns in your document in-between the chapters.

Inserting the Page Break as described, begins your next Chapter at the Top of the Next page. When readers click on a Chapter Title in your Table of Contents they are hyperlinked directly to the Top of the Page where the Chapter rightly begins.

Note: To test if you've done this right, when you see white space in your document (in between chapters), click anywhere on the white space, it should take your curser to the end of the proceeding chapter.

If this doesn't happen, and your cursor appears in the white-space, then you have extra Hard Returns in between the chapters.

Tap your back key (delete key) erasing the Hard Returns until you arrive at the end of the proceeding chapter. This streamlines your document, and makes it easier for Kindle to upload your eBook without issues, making your upload experience trouble free.

Step 11: Inserting Headers 1, and Headers 2

For Chapter Titles, and other major wording which you want larger in the text, don't use the normal Size function such as changing the Size of characters from 12 pt. to 18 pt. Instead, highlight your titles, and select Header 1, or Header 2 from your Styles function.

Use the Header 1, and Header 2, styles in your "View Styles Drawer" to highlight your Chapter Titles, and any Sub-Headings in your Text. Header 1 for the Chapter Titles. Header 2 for any Sub titles in the body of your chapter.

Kindle recognizes these "Styles" and offers you a way to standardize the titles in your document which are readable by Kindle.

Kindle supports basic character, and word, formatting such as Bold, Italic, and indents, so you have some flexibility in your character, and word formats.

Step 12: Hyperlinks and Bookmarks - building your Table of Contents

A major difference between Print books, and eBooks is the hyperlink. E-books are dynamic, meaning you can add links in your text which operate as "buttons" taking the reader to another part of your book, or to some website outside your book.

As you build your Table of Content you'll add Hyperlinks from each Chapter Title to the Chapter location in your eBook (called a Bookmark).

Bookmarks in your document tell the computer the destinations in your text you want to link to such as Chapter Titles. To make your Bookmark list, first, scroll down your document. Highlight anything you wish to Bookmark in your text, such as Chapter Titles, Sub-titles, or important Paragraphs (Note: you can only add Bookmarks one at a time).

In WORD, open your "Inspector" under VIEW in your format bar.

Highlight the Chapter Title you wish to Bookmark. Then, go to "Insert" on our format bar, and select "Insert - Hyperlink."

Once, you've selected Hyperlink for your highlighted text, your "inspector" window will give you a tab choice. Select Bookmark, and click the "+" tab at the bottom. The Chapter Title you highlighted is now entered in your list of Bookmarks (it will show on the list). Scroll down your your document and highlight, insert-hyperlink, click Bookmark, click "+" and keep adding, and building to your Bookmark list.

Once, all your individual Chapter Titles are entered into your Bookmark list, now it's time to build your Table of Contents.

Go to your Table of Contents page. Type a list of your Chapter Titles separated by Hard Returns in your Table of Contents page.

Highlight a Chapter Title, and select "Insert - Hyperlink" from your "Insert" function on your format bar. In your "Inspector window," select "Bookmark" under the "Link To:" prompt.

Once you select Bookmark, your list of previously set Bookmarks will appear (may be a pull-down menu with "none" in the tab window, until you click). Select the appropriate Chapter Title you see on the list.

Your hyperlink is now set. It's that easy. When you, or your reader, select the Chapter Title in the Table of Contents, they "hyperlink" directly to the beginning of the selected Chapter in your eBook.

If you wanted your Hyperlink to go to a website, outside of your eBook on the web, then in the last step select "Hyperlink". Your inspector window will change and you'll see a prompt to enter the formal URL of the website destination. Note: be sure to enter the website formally with http:// at the beginning.

Step 13: SAVING, and NAMING your WORD.doc file

Now, you've written your draft, and added your document formatting, its time to Save. Be sure to SAVE AS, and name a WORD.doc file. The next step, is to add any Images to your eBook. For this subject we go to the next Chapter: Importing, and formatting Images.

Chapter Five: Formatting Images

Graphics are a dynamic aspect of digital publishing. Images are optional in eBooks, other than the cover. You can use them, or not use them. Kindle publishing supports several Image Formats, however, for best results Always save Images in .JPEG format.

There are limits to how images and text are arranged on a page in the Kindle platform. Images can be placed (centered) above, or below text. And, conversely, text can be above, or below images.

Wrapping text around images is not supported, and will result, most likely, in formatting errors making your pages display in a way you didn't intend. And, be sure to "Center" your images in your document.

Images, are a special case with digital publishing, and require specific formatting to upload smoothly, and to display as you intend on a Mobile device.

Step 14: Importing Images

Formatting images properly in your WORD.doc document, if you're include images, is vital for digital publishing. Just as you must "think" like a computer "thinks" with your Title content, image processing is vitally important in terms of format, and size.

Any single Kindle page is 600 pixels wide, and 800 pixels tall. Be sure your image doesn't exceed this size, or the result won't be readable on a Kindle reader. Images you intend to include in your eBooks need to "Inserted" into documents using the "Insert" function in WORD.

For Mac publishers, Insert - Choose is the command to import an image. Insert - Picture if you're using older versions. The proper procedure is to use the Insert function in MS WORD. Insert Picture (or Insert - Choose - File Name) - command will allow you to chose an image to import into your WORD.doc document.

Note: Do Not use Cut-N-Paste to import images into your eBook draft document. It's important to avoid formatting errors when you include images in your eBook. Cut-N-Paste is not supported, and will result in formatting errors. Use the "Insert" function in Word to bring images into your eBook document.

Several image formats are supported by Kindle, but it is highly recommended you choose .JPEG images. The JPEG format works best, and will give you an excellent look on the Kindle, and other, devices which Kindle supports.

Step 15: Saving your Images as Compressed Files

The digital size of your eBook matters.

Amazon will charge a small digital delivery fee when your eBook is purchased, and downloaded. Therefore, you want your images, and therefore, document files to be as small as possible in the final SAVE AS for your eBook file.

Use the "image compression" function you'll find on Word Image Format bar.

Chapter Six - Creating your eBook Cover

Urban Wind
Vertical Axis Wind Turbines

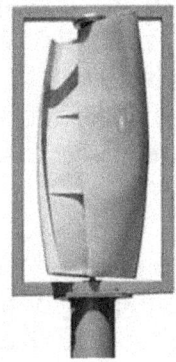

Wind Power in the City
Christopher Kinkaid

After your Content, Title and Sub-Title, your eBook Cover is the most important aspect of your digital eBook. Cover graphics are exciting, and challenging. Some people respond to subtle images, and others react to loud graphics. In reality, your eBook cover will be a synthesis of what you want to see, and what tools and resources are available to pull it off.

Step 16: Creating your eBook Cover

Producing your eBook cover is an important step.

Essentially, you have three choices in approaching the production of your eBook cover:

First, you can do it yourself, and learn the techniques to use a graphics program like PhotoShop, Illustrator, or other graphics program which can save files as a .JPEG. Producing your eBook cover yourself is a great way to have absolute "creative control." And, producing your own eBook cover images has the lowest cost to the author, and/or publisher.

Creating your eBook cover is really fun. You'll see your concepts take graphic form, and once you see your Cover taking shape, you'll be delighted. It's really the most fun, other than seeing your first sale!

Another way, and the easiest way to produce a great looking eBook cover is to use some of the Amazon tools for publishers.

Amazon has an eBook cover generator on your Bookshelf page. Use this program as your writing your book to play with different eBook covers. After you enter your eBook title, sub-title, and author on your Bookshelf page, click the eBook generator wizard, and play around with different designs, and layouts.

The Amazon eBook cover generator will take your Title, Sub-Title, and Author information entered under your NEW TITLE, and offer you a variety, though somewhat limited, gallery of images you can use worldwide and license free. Play with this eBook Cover generator for playing with ideas, and different layouts.

Note: Save as Draft until you've decided on your final eBook Cover design.

Second, you could "outsource" your eBook cover, and have someone else do it. There are services, and service outlets, such as fiverr which offer very cost-effective eBook Cover design services you can purchase at reasonable prices. The important issue is to Own Worldwide Rights to your text and images.

Your Third option is a hybrid of the first two. The best way, is to take the time to design your own eBook covers, and use the resources, such as those above, to bring your eBook to life, and saved as a .JPEG file. You want your eBook cover to be intriguing, vibrant, eye-catching, and most of all, exciting to the Reader.

Purchasing HD images from sources such as fotolia is a great resource for vibrant graphics you can use on your eBook cover. When you register with fotolia you can download images with Worldwide Royalty Free license, typically for a small fee. After you download your images, you can import them into your Graphics program and begin editing, and adding your Title, Sub-title, and Author information.

For eBook Cover image ideas, search foltolia, with their 27 million plus HD graphics. This kind of graphics data base will give you many useful and dynamic possibilities for your eBook cover design, and ideas will flow.

Chapter Seven: The Importance of an Editor

The greatest bit of advice I can offer an author, before publishing, is seek out an editor. An editor, is not just someone who may be an "expert" in the field you're writing about, but rather, an example of your typical reader.

Writing is complex on so many levels. Having more eyes on your writing is invaluable. You're not looking for a rewrite with an editor. You're looking for production notes. How does the eBook read? Is your eBook easy to Navigate?

You're looking for "feedback" on any, and all, aspects of the reader's experience, phrasing, pace, sentence structure. Spell checker software can identify most spelling issues, but phrasing, sentence content, and cadence are vital for best results, and humans are best for "fleshing" out edits.

Step 17: Read your eBook, as your Reader

As you write your eBook you will have edits, additions, and rewrites. As you write your eBook, there will a point you reach which *seems* to be the end of the eBook: your first Draft.

Usually, a writer is so engrossed in the eBook they're writing it's easy to loose some perspective. By the time you reach the end of your eBook, and as you begin your Start-to-Finish read throughs, take a day off from your eBook, then return and read your eBook from the perspective of your prospective Reader. I guarantee a day off, and you'll find a few more tweaks to your manuscript.

Is your eBook easy to read? Enjoyable to read? These subtle aspects will reveal themselves as you re-read your eBook. It takes several final reads, but going through your eBook start to finish as a reader is a great way to finely settle on your final form.

Chapter Eight: Uploading your Document and Going Live

Uploading your eBook is the moment of truth.

Your've written your eBook Chapters. You've written your Elements including "About the Author." You've finally formatted your WORD document, and inserted any images you may wish to include.

You've built your Table of Contents, and inserted all the hyperlinks, going to either Websites outside your eBook, or Bookmarks anywhere in your document.

You've had your document read by someone for some feedback. A knowledgable editor is preferred, but all readers bring valuable feedback.

And, you've SAVE AS, in a Compressed File format. Your eBook is almost ready to launch on the world.

Step 18: Confirm your eBook with a Final Read Through, and Check List

You've checked, and double checked that all "extraneous" hard-returns, and space bars spaces have been removed from your document. You want your WORD.doc to be clean with no extraneous bits.

The text in your document is built with, hard returns, headers 1, or 2 for titles. All page breaks inserted at the end of each Chapter to separate chapters. All bookmarks, and hyperlinks installed, and tested, such as your Table of Contents.

All images saved in .JPEG format, and Compressed for small file size. A "Clean Copy" of your WORD.doc will make the upload very easy.

Now, you're ready to Go Live on the Amazon platform in the following step. You're 10 steps away from Launch.

Step 19: Setting up your Publishing Account with Kindle, and Uploading your eBook

To go live on the worldwide web with your eBook on the Kindle, use the following steps:

Step One: Confirm the Content of your eBook is saved in a WORD.doc file, and your Cover image saved in a separate .JPEG file. SAVE AS, to your desktop, or folder, as described above.

Step Two: Set-up your Account on Kindle Publishing

Step Three: Go to your Amazon "BookShelf" page, and click New Title

Step *Four*: Once you're selected New Title on your Bookshelf, enter your "Front Matter" information including Title, Sub-Title, Author, and any other contributors as prompted. Enter up to 7 Keywords, and select up to 2 Categories offered under the selections available, and enter a "Description" of your eBook. The "Description" page will be displayed on the Amazon sales page.

Step Five: Create an eBook Cover with the Amazon Wizard (you'll see the prompt), or Upload your own eBook Cover .JPEG file.

Step Six: Select Save As Draft

Step Seven: Upload your eBook document. Select eBook Upload, and click on your .doc file name at the prompt. Click "upload," and you're on your way.

*Step Eigh*t: After you Upload your eBook .doc file, and your eBook Cover image .JPEG file, and entered all of your eBook "Front Matter" information, then you select pricing for your eBook.

Pricing is an important aspect to the Commercial side of your eBook, so I'm devoting a Chapter to the topic. Please see Chapter Nine: Monetization. Once you've selected the sales price for your eBook in various countries, you're ready for the Big Moment. The moment you go live worldwide.

Step Nine: Click SAVE and SUBMIT, and your file will upload to Amazon

Step Ten: Amazon will require 12 to 48 hours to process your uploaded files into the format supported by Mobile Devices. Amazon converts your submitted files into .MOBI format, and within hours, you're live - worldwide - on the Amazon platform!

Congratulations! You're now a Published eBook Author on Amazon!

Chapter Nine: Monetization

Digital publishing has a monetary aspect. Digital downloads of your eBook can be offered for free, or you can charge per copy. The choice is yours. If you decide to sell your eBook, Amazon has made it easy to enter the pricing you select.

If you choose to charge a fee for your eBook, then you must address monetization. Simply stated, how much do you want to charge for your eBook?

Pricing on the Kindle platform is determined by the scope of your Copyrights, and by country. You can set your US price in Dollars per eBook, and if you own worldwide rights to your eBook, you can use this price for all markets, or select different prices for different countries.

Amazon presently has two pricing structures for Author royalties. You can earn 35%, or 70% of your selling price, depending on the price you choose for your eBook, and varies from country to country as well.

If you price your eBook on Amazon below $2.99, then you'll earn 35% royalty on sales.

If you price your ebook between $2.99 and $9.99 each, then you'll earn 70% royalty.

If you price your eBook above $9.99 then your royalty goes back to 35% of sales.

Pricing your eBook is a tricky question. As a general rule, lower prices tend to sell more eBooks than higher prices. However, my experience shows there is a difference between FICTION, and NON FICTION eBook pricing.

Non-fiction eBooks can command a higher price, and sometimes are judged by "you get what you pay for" attitudes.

Fiction eBooks, on the other hand, are best in lower range. The most popular pricing, in my research, sets prices for these eBooks between $1.99 to $5.99 each, with the maxima on $2.99 to $3.99.

Digital publishing for profit is a numbers game. The best result seems to be a balance between more sales, with less margin, producing more overall income, than smaller sales of lower volume with higher margins. A balance in all things. Fortunately, with the Kindle platform you can change your pricing at any time, and this gives you an opportunity to "play" with pricing to find your eBooks sweet spot.

After a 60 day initial period, Amazon pays monthly if you reach an undisclosed "minimum" volume of sales. You can specify being sent a monthly check, or EFT electronic fund transfer automatically to your bank account. Amazon makes these options easy to select, and execute.

Chapter Ten: Building your Brand

Digital publishing gives you enormous reach. In the old days, marketing required a great deal of resources. Digital publishing gives you tools which make you a powerful publisher to a worldwide audience, directly from your Computer.

Building your Brand is all about marketing your eBooks built on a foundation of your Web Presence. Amazon has developed tools for authors, and publishers, which you should take advantage of in your publishing business plan.

Amazon offers Author Pages for each of their platforms around the world. After you publish your first book, Amazon will send you an invitation by email to sign up for Amazon's other international platforms. Click the links in the email, and sign up for Amazon's author tools, and web presence.

Publishing to Amazon is just the beginning, though a good one, to worldwide publishing. After you publish your eBook, you may consider printing some "Hard copy" versions of your eBook.

There are additional steps you can take in building your brand on the web. You can offer your "hard copy" version, on demand, printed one by one, with CreateSpace, for example. Barnes & Noble is another great outlet for distribution.

Register a URL using your Title Name for a website you can build dedicated to your eBook. The website, with your eBook Title as the URL, would work as a marketing tool. On your eBook titled website you can build a link (download the code from Amazon) to bring people to the Amazon store for purchasing your eBook.

Also, there is software you can download from third parties which allow you to Manage a PDF download of your eBook from your website. However, use caution, that you always stay within Amazon rules, so study everything Amazon says about these topics.

Note: Building a dedicated website has hosting costs. One advantage of publishing on Amazon, there are no costs.

On Amazon platforms, your eBook can earn, throughout time, with no overhead costs, making digital publishing unparalleled in potential return on investment. All, or most, of your work is on the front-end of your publishing project.

If you work the "back-end," of publishing, you can increase your sales dramatically by tapping additional distribution channels. Once your eBook is published, you can schedule Radio interviews, lectures, write Press-Releases, and other out-reach activities to increase publicity, and exposure to your eBook.

Chapter Eleven: Publish Foreign Language Translations of your eBook as Separate eBooks

Everyone has a native language. Translating your eBook into foreign languages is one method of increasing your worldwide reach, and increasing your readers pleasure.

There many ways to approach translation, and as language is involved, a very delicate proposition in eBook publishing. However, translating your eBook makes great sense from a marketing, and branding point of view, and can be very effective.

Translation is best done by a literate native speaker. If you don't have a native speaker in the language you're interested in translating, another option is hiring a service.

Another method for translation of Word Documents to another language is to use "mechanical" software. Use translating software with Great care.

Using "mechanical" translators are excellent for a first draft purposes, but are best used in combination with a native speaker. Translating software has yet to catch the true subtlety of language, so translations are delicate, and require great attention.

Google offers some tools for translation, and may be a good starting point. In the Kindle platform foreign language translations of your eBook are considered separate eBooks. Be sure to secure ALL copyrights in writing, to your translations, if you use third party translators.

Chapter Twelve: Overview and Quick Guide

Publishing your eBook on Amazon's worldwide Kindle platform is powerful, satisfying, and potentially profitable. Below are listed the 19 Steps you can follow to produce vibrant, dynamic, and successful eBooks, published on the Amazon Kindle platform, for worldwide distribution, and sales.

Use the steps below to take your eBook publishing from Concept to Cash-flow.

Step 1: Table of Contents

Step 2: Preface

Step 3: About the Book

Step 4: About the Author

Step 5: Introduction

Step 6: Chapters

Step 7: Epilogue

Step 8: Titles and Sub-Titles

Step 9: Formatting your WORD.doc

Step 10: Inserting Page Breaks

Step 11: Inserting Headers 1 and 2

Step 12: Hyperlinks and Bookmarks

Step 13: Saving and Naming your files

Step 14: Formatting Images

Step 15: Compressing File Sizes

Step 16: Creating your eBook Cover

Step 17: Editing your eBook

Step 18: Final Check List and Review

Step 19: Upload to Amazon

There you have it future eBook author.

The Steps outlined above are your road-map to eBook publishing on Amazon. These are the tools you need to bring your eBook from your computer, into the leading worldwide sales platform on the web, and generate income.

Kindle publishing gives you the most powerful platform for earning royalties, and reaching out to the world with your content. I know you're going to enjoy checking your Amazon reports, and seeing how many times around the world your eBook is purchased, and enjoyed.

May your publishing experience be as rewarding as I've found, and I hope this Book has been a useful resource for your digital publishing projects.

Thank you for reading, and happy publishing on Amazon Kindle!